# Diaper Cover Sets

Could babies get any cuter? Yes, when you dress them in fun outfits like these! The whimsical sets are easy to create by using different yarn colors and embellishments for special hats and a basic diaper cover and booties (patterns on pages 2 and 3). In sizes up to 12 months, the designs are knit using medium weight yarn.

LEISURE ARTS, INC. • Maumelle, Arkansas

# BASIC DIAPER COVER

**◼◼◻◻◻ EASY +**

See the Shopping List for the set you are making.

## SIZE INFORMATION

**Finished Size:**

**0-3 Months**
15" waist x 6¾" high (38 cm x 17 cm)

**3-6 Months**
16" waist x 7¾" high
   (40.5 cm x 19.5 cm)

**6-12 Months**
17" waist x 9" high (43 cm x 23 cm)

*Size Note:* We have printed the instructions for the sizes in different colors to make it easier for you to find:
• 0-3 Months in Blue
• 3-6 Months in Pink
• 6-12 Months in Green
Instructions in Black apply to all sizes.

## GAUGE INFORMATION

With medium size straight needles, in Stockinette Stitch (knit one row, purl one row),
   18 sts and 28 rows = 4" (10 cm)

## TECHNIQUES USED

◼ YO *(Fig. 3, page 29)*
◼ Add on New Stitches *(Figs. 4a & b, page 29)*
◼ Knit in front and back increase *(Figs. 5a & b, page 29)*
◼ K2 tog *(Fig. 6, page 29)*

## INSTRUCTIONS

### BODY (Make 2)

**SHAPING**

With medium size straight needles, Main Color, and leaving a long end for sewing, cast on 14{16-18} sts.

**Row 1** (Right side)**:** Knit across.

**Row 2:** Purl across.

Repeat Rows 1 and 2 for Stockinette Stitch, 1{2-3} time(s).

**Increase Row:** Knit in front and back of first st, knit across to last st, knit in front and back of last st: 16{18-20} sts.

Continue to increase every other row, 6 times, ending by working a **purl** row: 28{30-32} sts.

**Next Row:** Add on 4 sts, knit across: 32{34-36} sts.

**Next Row:** Add on 4 sts, purl across: 36{38-40} sts.

Work even in Stockinette Stitch until Body measures 5½{6½-7½}"/ 14{16.5-19} cm from cast on edge, ending by working a **purl** row; cut Main Color.

### WAISTBAND

Change to smallest size straight needles.

**Rows 1 thru 4{4-6}:** With Contrasting Color, (K1, P1) across.

**Eyelet Row:** K2{3-4}, YO, K2 tog, (K2, YO, K2 tog) 3 times, K4, YO, K2 tog, (K2, YO, K2 tog) 3 times, K2{3-4}.

**Last 4 Rows:** (K1, P1) across.

Using largest size straight needle, bind off all sts in pattern.

## FINISHING

### EMBROIDERY

Follow the instructions for the Stars & Moon, Watermelon, Cow, or Butterfly & Clouds.

Using matching colors, ◼ weave side seams across ends of rows *(Fig. 8a, page 30)*, from added on stitches to bound off edge.

### LEG RIBBING

With **right** side facing, using smallest size straight needles and Contrasting Color, ◼ pick up 40{44-48} sts evenly spaced across Shaping *(Fig. 9a, page 30)*.

**Row 1:** (K1, P1) across.

Repeat Row 1, 6{6-8} times.

Using largest size straight needle, bind off all sts in pattern.

Repeat for second leg.

Using matching colors, ◼ weave bottom seam across cast on edge *(Figs. 8b & c, page 30)* and across Leg Ribbings.

## TIE

With double pointed needles and Main Color, cast on 2 sts.

Make an 🎥 I-Cord as follows:
★ Without turning the needle, slide the sts to the opposite end of the needle, K2; repeat from ★ until the I-Cord measures approximately 30{32-34}"/76{81.5-86.5} cm.

Bind off.

Beginning at center front, weave the Tie through Eyelet Row of the Waistband.

## BASIC BOOTIES

◼◼◻◻◻ **EASY +**

**See the Shopping List for the set you are making.**

## SIZE INFORMATION

| Size | Finished Sole Length |
|------|----------------------|
| 0-3 Months | 3½" (9 cm) |
| 3-6 Months | 4¼" (11 cm) |

*Size Note:* We have printed the instructions for the sizes in different colors to make it easier for you to find:
• 0-3 Months in Blue
• 3-6 Months in Pink
Instructions in Black apply to both sizes.

## GAUGE INFORMATION

With medium size straight needles, in Stockinette Stitch (knit one row, purl one row),
    9 sts and 14 rows = 2" (5 cm)

## TECHNIQUE USED

🎥 K2 tog *(Fig. 6, page 29)*

## INSTRUCTIONS
### BODY

With medium size straight needles and Main Color, cast on 22{24} sts.

Work in Stockinette Stitch for 3{3¾}"/7.5{9.5} cm, ending by working a **purl** row.

## TOE SHAPING

**Row 1:** K1, K2 tog across to last st, K1: 12{13} sts.

**Row 2:** Purl across.

**Size 0-3 Months Only - Row 3:** K1, K2 tog across to last st, K1: 7 sts.

**Size 3-6 Months Only - Row 3:** K1, K2 tog across: 7 sts.

Cut yarn leaving a long end for sewing. Thread the yarn needle with the end and slip the remaining sts onto the yarn needle and yarn; pull tightly to close. 🎥 Weave instep seam across end of rows 1½{1¾}"/4{4.5} cm from toe *(Fig. 8a, page 30)*.

## CUFF

With **right** side facing, medium size straight needle, and Main Color, 🎥 pick up 20{22} sts evenly spaced across end of rows *(Fig. 9a, page 30)*.

**Row 1:** (K1, P1) across.

Repeat Row 1, 5{7} times.

Cut Main Color leaving a long end for sewing.

With Contrasting Color, work in K1, P1 ribbing for 2 rows.

With largest size straight needle, bind off all sts in pattern; cut yarn leaving a long end for sewing.

## FINISHING
### EMBROIDERY

Follow the instructions for the Stars & Moon, Watermelon, Cow, or Butterfly & Clouds.

Using matching colors, weave back seam across end of rows on Cuff and 🎥 cast on edges on Body *(Figs. 8b & c, page 30)* to within ½" (1.25 cm) of the heel. Flatten the heel and sew the sts together.

Repeat for the second bootie.

# Stars & Moon

**EASY +**

## SHOPPING LIST

**Yarn** (Medium Weight) **4** MEDIUM
**[1.75 ounces, 80 yards
(50 grams, 73 meters) per skein]:**
- ☐ Main Color (Navy) - 2{3-3} skeins
- ☐ Contrasting Color (White) -
  1 skein
- ☐ Stars (Yellow) - small amount

## Knitting Needles

Straight,
- ☐ Size 6 (4 mm),
- ☐ Size 7 (4.5 mm) **and**
- ☐ Size 10 (6 mm) (for binding off)

Double pointed (2),
- ☐ size 3 (3.25 mm) for Moon

Double pointed (set of 5),
- ☐ Size 7 (4.5 mm)

16" (40.5 cm) Circular,
- ☐ Size 7 (4.5 mm)
  **or** sizes needed for gauge

## Additional Supplies

- ☐ Split ring marker
- ☐ Yarn needle

# DIAPER COVER

Work same as Basic Diaper Cover, page 2.

## EMBROIDERY

Using photo as a guide for placement, Yellow, and  straight stitch (*Fig. 10, page 31*), embroider stars on back of Body using 4 stitches for each star.

# BOOTIES

Work same as Basic Booties, page 3.

## EMBROIDERY

Using photo as a guide for placement, Yellow, and straight stitch (*Fig. 10, page 31*), embroider stars on Body and Toe Shaping using 3 stitches for each star.

# HAT
## SIZE INFORMATION

| Size | Finished Circumference | |
|------|------------|--------|
| 0-3 Months | 12½" | (32 cm) |
| 3-6 Months | 14¼" | (36 cm) |
| 6-12 Months | 16" | (40.5 cm) |

*Size Note:* We have printed the instructions for the sizes in different colors to make it easier for you to find:

• 0-3 Months in Blue

• 3-6 Months in Pink

• 6-12 Months in Green

Instructions in Black apply to all sizes.

## GAUGE INFORMATION

With circular needle, in Stockinette Stitch (knit each rnd),
    18 sts and 28 rnds = 4" (10 cm)

## TECHNIQUES USED

Add on new stitches (*Figs. 4a & b, page 29*)

K2 tog (*Fig. 6, page 29*)

P2 tog (*Fig. 7, page 29*)

## INSTRUCTIONS
### BODY

With 🎥 circular needle and Navy, cast on 56{64-72} sts (*Fig. 1, page 28*); 🎥 place a marker to indicate the beginning of the round (*see Markers, page 28*).

Knit each rnd until piece measures approximately 5{5½-6}"/ 12.5{14-15} cm from cast on edge with edge flat; Body will be shorter when cast on edge is allowed to roll.

### SHAPING

Change to larger size 🎥 double pointed needles (*Fig. 2, page 28*) when there are too few stitches to use the circular needle.

**Rnd 1:** (K6, K2 tog) around: 49{56-63} sts.

**Rnd 2:** Knit around.

**Rnd 3:** (K5, K2 tog) around: 42{48-54} sts.

**Rnd 4:** Knit around.

**Rnd 5:** (K4, K2 tog) around: 35{40-45} sts.

**Rnds 6-8:** Knit around.

**Rnd 9:** (K3, K2 tog) around: 28{32-36} sts.

### SIZE 0-3 MONTHS ONLY
**Rnds 10-12:** Knit around.

**Rnd 13:** (K2, K2 tog) around: 21 sts.

**Rnds 14-16:** Knit around.

**Rnd 17:** (K1, K2 tog) around: 14 sts.

**Rnds 18-20:** Knit around.

**Rnd 21:** K2 tog around: 7 sts.

**Rnds 22-24:** Knit around.

**Rnd 25:** K1, K2 tog around: 4 sts.

### SIZES 3-6 & 6-12 MONTHS ONLY
**Rnds 10-13:** Knit around.

**Rnd 14:** (K2, K2 tog) around: {24-27} sts.

**Rnds 15-18:** Knit around.

**Rnd 19:** (K1, K2 tog) around: {16-18} sts.

**Rnds 20-23:** Knit around.

**Rnd 24:** K2 tog around: {8-9} sts.

**Rnds 25-28:** Knit around.

### SIZE 3-6 MONTHS ONLY
**Rnd 29:** K2 tog around: 4 sts.

### SIZE 6-12 MONTHS ONLY
**Rnd 29:** K1, K2 tog around: 5 sts.

**Rnd 30:** K2 tog, K3: 4 sts.

### ALL SIZES
Slip remaining 4 sts onto one double pointed needle.

Make an 🎥 I-Cord as follows:
★ Without turning the needle, slide the sts to the opposite end of the needle, K4; repeat from ★ until the I-Cord measures approximately 2{2½-3}"/5{6.5-7.5} cm.

Cut yarn leaving a long end for sewing. 🎥 To gather the remaining sts, thread the yarn needle with the end and slip the remaining sts onto the yarn needle and yarn, pull tightly to close the hole and secure end; insert needle down through the center of the I-Cord to hide end.

### EMBROIDERY
Using photo as a guide for placement, Yellow, and 🎥 straight stitch (*Fig. 10, page 31*), embroider stars on Body and Shaping using 3 or 4 stitches for each star.

# MOON

## FIRST HALF

With smaller size double pointed needles and White, cast on 2 sts.

**Row 1** (Right side)**:** Knit across.

**Row 2:** Purl across.

**Row 3:** Knit across.

**Row 4** (Increase row)**:** Add on one st, purl across: 3 sts.

**Rows 5-10:** Repeat Rows 1-4 once, then repeat Rows 1 and 2 once **more**: 4 sts.

**Row 11:** Knit across.

**Row 12:** Purl across.

**Row 13:** Knit across.

**Row 14** (Decrease row)**:** P2 tog, purl across: 3 sts.

**Rows 15-21:** Repeat Rows 11-14 once, then repeat Rows 11-13 once **more**: 2 sts.

Cut yarn leaving a long end for sewing; pull end through remaining 2 sts.

## SECOND HALF

With smaller size double pointed needles and White, cast on 2 sts.

**Row 1:** Purl across.

**Row 2** (Right side)**:** Knit across.

**Row 3:** Purl across.

**Row 4** (Increase row)**:** Add on one st, knit across: 3 sts.

**Rows 5-10:** Repeat Rows 1-4 once, then repeat Rows 1 and 2 once **more**: 4 sts.

**Row 11:** Purl across.

**Row 12:** Knit across.

**Row 13:** Purl across.

**Row 14** (Decrease row)**:** K2 tog, knit across: 3 sts.

**Rows 15-21:** Repeat Rows 11-14 once, then repeat Rows 11-13 once **more**: 2 sts.

Cut yarn leaving a long end for sewing; pull end through remaining 2 sts.

With **right** sides together, sew around Halves to join; sew the Moon to the tip of the I-Cord.

# Watermelon

**◼◼◻◻** EASY +

## SHOPPING LIST

--------------------------------

### Yarn (Medium Weight) 🧶 **4** MEDIUM
**[1.75 ounces, 80 yards
(50 grams, 73 meters) per skein]:**

☐ Main Color (Red) - 2{3-3} skeins

☐ Contrasting Color (Green) -
1 skein

☐ Stripe (White) - small amount

☐ Seeds (Black) - small amount

### Knitting Needles
Straight,

☐ Size 6 (4 mm),

☐ Size 7 (4.5 mm) **and**

☐ Size 10 (6 mm) (for binding off)

Double pointed (set of 5),

☐ Size 7 (4.5 mm)

16" (40.5 cm) Circular,

☐ Size 7 (4.5 mm)

**or** sizes needed for gauge

### Additional Supplies

☐ Split ring marker

☐ Yarn needle

# DIAPER COVER

Work same as Basic Diaper Cover, page 2.

Using photo as a guide for placement, Black, and  duplicate stitch *(Figs. 13a & b, page 31)*, randomly add seeds to the front and back of the Body.

# BOOTIES

Work same as Basic Booties, page 3.

Using photo as a guide for placement, Black, and duplicate stitch *(Figs. 13a & b, page 31)*, randomly add seeds to the Body and Toe Shaping.

# HAT
## SIZE INFORMATION

| Size | Finished Circumference |
|------|------------------------|
| **0-3 Months** | 12½" (32 cm) |
| **3-6 Months** | 14¼" (36 cm) |
| **6-12 Months** | 16" (40.5 cm) |

*Size Note:* We have printed the instructions for the sizes in different colors to make it easier for you to find:

• 0-3 Months in Blue

• 3-6 Months in Purple

• 6-12 Months in Green

Instructions in Black apply to all sizes.

# GAUGE INFORMATION

With circular needle,
in Stockinette Stitch (knit each rnd),
    18 sts and 28 rnds = 4" (10 cm)

# TECHNIQUE USED

K2 tog *(Fig. 6, page 29)*

# INSTRUCTIONS

## BODY

With 🎥 circular needle and Green, cast on 56{64-72} sts (**Fig. 1, page 28**); 🎥 place a marker to indicate the beginning of the round (**see Markers, page 28**).

Knit 9{11-13} rnds.

Cut Green; with White, knit 4{6-8} rnds.

Cut White; with Red, knit each rnd until piece measures approximately 5{5½-6}"/12.5{14-15} cm from cast on edge with edge flat; Body will be shorter when cast on edge is allowed to roll.

## SHAPING

Change to 🎥 double pointed needles (**Fig. 2, page 28**) when there are too few stitches to use the circular needle.

**Rnd 1:** (K6, K2 tog) around: 49{56-63} sts.

**Rnd 2:** Knit around.

**Rnd 3:** (K5, K2 tog) around: 42{48-54} sts.

**Rnd 4:** Knit around.

**Rnd 5:** (K4, K2 tog) around: 35{40-45} sts.

**Rnd 6:** Knit around.

**Rnd 7:** (K3, K2 tog) around: 28{32-36} sts.

**Rnd 8:** Knit around.

**Rnd 9:** (K2, K2 tog) around: 21{24-27} sts.

**Rnd 10:** Knit around.

**Rnd 11:** (K1, K2 tog) around: 14{16-18} sts.

**Rnd 12:** K2 tog around: 7{8-9} sts.

Cut yarn leaving a long end for sewing. 🎥 To gather the remaining sts, thread the yarn needle with the end and slip the remaining sts onto the yarn needle and yarn; pull tightly to close the hole and secure end.

Using photo as a guide for placement, Black, and 🎥 duplicate stitch (**Figs. 13a & b, page 31**), randomly add seeds to the Body and Shaping.

# Cow

 **EASY +**

## SHOPPING LIST

- - - - - - - - - - - - - - - - - - - - - - - - - - - -

### Yarn (Medium Weight)
[1.75 ounces, 80 yards
(50 grams, 73 meters) per skein]:
☐ Main Color (White) -
   2{3-3} skeins
☐ Contrasting Color (Black) -
   1 skein

### Knitting Needles
Straight,
☐ Size 6 (4 mm),
☐ Size 7 (4.5 mm) **and**
☐ Size 10 (6 mm) (for binding off )
Double pointed (set of 5),
☐ Size 7 (4.5 mm)
16" (40.5 cm) Circular,
☐ Size 7 (4.5 mm)
   **or** sizes needed for gauge

### Additional Supplies
☐ Split ring marker
☐ Yarn needle

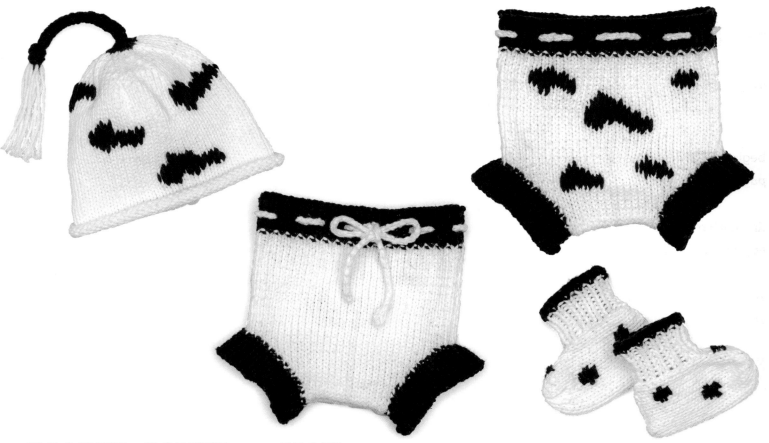

# DIAPER COVER

Work same as Basic Diaper Cover, page 2.

## EMBROIDERY

Using photo as a guide for placement, Black, and 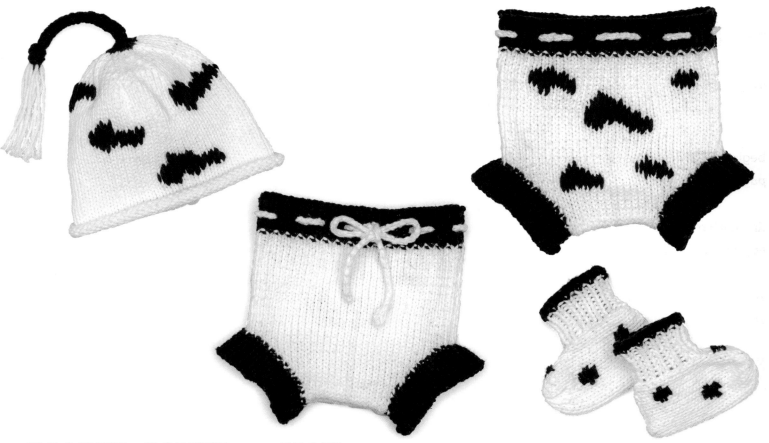 satin stitch (**Fig. 11, page 31**), embroider 5 different size patches on back of Body.

# BOOTIES

Work same as Basic Booties, page 3.

## EMBROIDERY

Using photo as a guide for placement, Black, and satin stitch (**Fig. 11, page 31**), embroider 5 different size patches around Body and Toe Shaping.

# HAT
## SIZE INFORMATION

| Size | Finished Circumference | |
|---|---|---|
| 0-3 Months | 12½" | (32 cm) |
| 3-6 Months | 14¼" | (36 cm) |
| 6-12 Months | 16" | (40.5 cm) |

*Size Note:* We have printed the instructions for the sizes in different colors to make it easier for you to find:
• 0-3 Months in Blue
• 3-6 Months in Pink
• 6-12 Months in Green
Instructions in Black apply to all sizes.

# GAUGE INFORMATION

With circular needle, in Stockinette Stitch (knit each rnd), 18 sts and 28 rnds = 4" (10 cm)

# TECHNIQUE USED

K2 tog (**Fig. 6, page 29**)

# INSTRUCTIONS
## BODY

With  circular needle and White, cast on 56{64-72} sts *(Fig. 1, page 28)*; place a marker to indicate the beginning of the round *(see Markers, page 28)*.

Knit each rnd until piece measures approximately 5{5½-6}"/ 12.5{14-15} cm from cast on edge with edge flat; Body will be shorter when cast on edge is allowed to roll.

## SHAPING

Change to double pointed needles *(Fig. 2, page 28)* when there are too few stitches to use the circular needle.

**Rnd 1:** (K6, K2 tog) around: 49{56-63} sts.

**Rnd 2:** Knit around.

**Rnd 3:** (K5, K2 tog) around: 42{48-54} sts.

**Rnd 4:** Knit around.

**Rnd 5:** (K4, K2 tog) around: 35{40-45} sts.

**Rnd 6:** Knit around.

**Rnd 7:** (K3, K2 tog) around: 28{32-36} sts.

**Rnd 8:** Knit around.

**Rnd 9:** (K2, K2 tog) around: 21{24-27} sts.

**Rnd 10:** Knit around; cut White.

**Rnd 11:** With Black, (K1, K2 tog) around: 14{16-18} sts.

**Rnd 12:** K2 tog around: 7{8-9} sts.

**SIZE 0-3 MONTHS ONLY**
**Rnd 13:** K1, K2 tog around: 4 sts.

**SIZE 3-6 MONTHS ONLY**
**Rnd 13:** K2 tog around: 4 sts.

**SIZE 6-12 MONTHS ONLY**
**Rnd 13:** K1, K2 tog around: 5 sts.

**ALL SIZES**
Slip remaining sts onto one double pointed needle.

Make an I-Cord as follows:
★ Without turning the needle, slide the sts to the opposite end of the needle, K4{4-5}; repeat from ★ until the I-Cord measures approximately 5{6-7}"/12.5{15-18} cm from cast on edge.

Cut yarn leaving a long end for sewing.

Cut 8{8-10} strands of White, each 12" (30.5 cm) long.

To add the strands to the I-Cord, hold 2 strands of White together and insert them through the first st. Fold the strands in half and remove the st from the needle *(Fig. A)*.

Fig. A

Repeat for each stitch.

Pull the Black yarn end to tighten the sts. Thread the yarn needle with the end and secure; insert needle down through the center of the I-Cord to hide end.

Tie the end of the I-Cord in a knot.

## EMBROIDERY

Using photo as a guide for placement, Black, and satin stitch *(Fig. 11, page 31)*, embroider different size patches around the Body.

# Butterfly & Clouds

■■□▷ **EASY +**

## SHOPPING LIST

------------------------------

### Yarn (Medium Weight) 🏷4
**[1.75 ounces, 80 yards
(50 grams, 73 meters) per skein]:**
- ☐ Main Color (Blue) - 2{3-3} skeins
- ☐ Contrasting Color (White) -
  1 skein
- ☐ Wings (Yellow) - small amount
- ☐ Antennae (Black) - small amount
  (Super Bulky Weight Novelty) 🏷6
- ☐ Clouds (White) - small amount

### Knitting Needles
Straight,
- ☐ Size 6 (4 mm),
- ☐ Size 7 (4.5 mm) **and**
- ☐ Size 10 (6 mm) (for binding off)
Double pointed (2),
- ☐ Size 6 (4 mm) for Butterfly
Double pointed (set of 5),
- ☐ Size 7 (4.5 mm)
16" (40.5 cm) Circular,
- ☐ Size 7 (4.5 mm)
  or sizes needed for gauge

### Additional Supplies
- ☐ Split ring marker
- ☐ Yarn needle

# DIAPER COVER

Work same as Basic Diaper Cover, page 2.

## EMBROIDERY

Using photo as a guide for placement, Novelty yarn, and  satin stitch *(Fig. 11, page 31)*, embroider 5 different size clouds on back of Body.

# BOOTIES

Work same as Basic Booties, page 3.

## EMBROIDERY

Using photo as a guide for placement, Novelty yarn, and satin stitch *(Fig. 11, page 31)*, embroider 4 different size clouds around Body and Toe Shaping.

# HAT
## SIZE INFORMATION

| Size | Finished Circumference | |
|---|---|---|
| 0-3 Months | 12½" | (32 cm) |
| 3-6 Months | 14¼" | (36 cm) |
| 6-12 Months | 16" | (40.5 cm) |

*Size Note:* We have printed the instructions for the sizes in different colors to make it easier for you to find:

• 0-3 Months in Blue

• 3-6 Months in Pink

• 6-12 Months in Green

Instructions in Black apply to all sizes.

15

## GAUGE INFORMATION

With circular needle,

in Stockinette Stitch (knit each rnd),

18 sts and 28 rnds = 4" (10 cm)

## TECHNIQUES USED

📹 Knit in front and back increase
*(Figs. 5a & b, page 29)*

📹 K2 tog *(Fig. 6, page 29)*

## INSTRUCTIONS
### BODY

With 📹 circular needle and Blue, cast on 56{64-72} sts *(Fig. 1, page 28)*; 📹 place a marker to indicate the beginning of the round *(see Markers, page 28)*.

Knit each rnd until piece measures approximately 5{5½-6}"/ 12.5{14-15} cm from cast on edge with edge flat; Body will be shorter when cast on edge is allowed to roll.

### SHAPING

Change to larger size 📹 double pointed needles *(Fig. 2, page 28)* when there are too few stitches to use the circular needle.

**Rnd 1:** (K6, K2 tog) around: 49{56-63} sts.

**Rnd 2:** Knit around.

**Rnd 3:** (K5, K2 tog) around: 42{48-54} sts.

**Rnd 4:** Knit around.

**Rnd 5:** (K4, K2 tog) around: 35{40-45} sts.

**Rnds 6-8:** Knit around.

**Rnd 9:** (K3, K2 tog) around: 28{32-36} sts.

**SIZE 0-3 MONTHS ONLY**
**Rnds 10-12:** Knit around.

**Rnd 13:** (K2, K2 tog) around: 21 sts.

**Rnds 14-16:** Knit around.

**Rnd 17:** (K1, K2 tog) around: 14 sts.

**Rnds 18-20:** Knit around.

**Rnd 21:** K2 tog around: 7 sts.

**Rnds 22-24:** Knit around.

**Rnd 25:** K1, K2 tog around: 4 sts.

**SIZES 3-6 & 6-12 MONTHS ONLY**
**Rnds 10-13:** Knit around.

**Rnd 14:** (K2, K2 tog) around: {24-27} sts.

**Rnds 15-18:** Knit around.

**Rnd 19:** (K1, K2 tog) around: {16-18} sts.

**Rnds 20-23:** Knit around.

**Rnd 24:** K2 tog around: {8-9} sts.

**Rnds 25-28:** Knit around.

**SIZE 3-6 MONTHS ONLY**
**Rnd 29:** K2 tog around: 4 sts.

**SIZE 6-12 MONTHS ONLY**
**Rnd 29:** K1, K2 tog around: 5 sts.

**Rnd 30:** K2 tog, K3: 4 sts.

**ALL SIZES**
Slip remaining 4 sts onto one double pointed needle.

Make an 📹 I-Cord as follows:
★ Without turning the needle, slide the sts to the opposite end of the needle, K4; repeat from ★ until the I-Cord measures approximately 2{2½-3}"/5{6.5-7.5} cm.

Cut yarn leaving a long end for sewing. 📹 To gather the remaining sts, thread the yarn needle with the end and slip the remaining sts onto the yarn needle and yarn, pull tightly to close the hole and secure end; insert needle down through the center of the I-Cord to hide end.

## EMBROIDERY

Using photo as a guide for placement, Novelty yarn, and 📹 satin stitch *(Fig. 11, page 31)*, embroider different size clouds around Body and Shaping.

# BUTTERFLY

**WING** (Make 2)

With smallest size straight needles and Yellow, cast on 7 sts.

**Rows 1 and 2:** Knit across.

**Row 3** (Increase row)**:** K1, knit in front and back of next st, knit across to last 2 sts, knit in front and back of next st, K1: 9 sts.

**Row 4:** Knit across.

**Rows 5-7:** Repeat Rows 3 and 4 once, then repeat Row 3 once **more**: 13 sts.

**Row 8:** K6, K2 tog, K5: 12 sts.

## First Tip

**Row 1** (Right side)**:** (K1, K2 tog) twice, leave remaining 6 sts on needle: 4 sts.

*Note:* Loop a short piece of yarn around any st on Row 1 to mark **right** side.

**Row 2:** Turn; K2 tog twice: 2 sts.

**Row 3:** K2 tog.

Cut yarn leaving a long end; pull end through st.

## Second Tip

**Row 1:** With **right** side facing, Yellow, and working across unworked sts, (K2 tog, K1) twice: 4 sts.

**Row 2:** K2 tog twice: 2 sts.

**Row 3:** K2 tog.

Cut yarn leaving a long end; pull end through st.

## BODY

With smaller size double pointed needles and Blue, cast on 2 sts.

Work I-Cord for 1½" (4 cm).

**Increase Row:** Knit in front and back of each st: 4 sts.

Cut yarn leaving a long end for sewing. Thread the yarn needle with the end and slip the remaining sts onto the yarn needle and yarn, pull tightly to close the hole and secure end; insert needle down through the center of the I-Cord to hide end.

Sew Wings together across the cast on edges. Sew the Body to the **right** side of the Wings across the seam.

Thread a short piece of Black through the end of the Body for the antennae and tie in a knot; trim ends to ½" (1.25 cm).

## EMBROIDERY

Using photo as a guide for placement, Blue, and  French knots *(Fig. 12, page 31)*, embroider 2 dots on each Wing.

Sew the top of the Butterfly to the end of the I-Cord.

# Bumble Bee

EASY +

## SHOPPING LIST

**Yarn** (Medium Weight) **4 MEDIUM**
**[1.75 ounces, 80 yards
(50 grams, 73 meters) per skein]:**
☐ Main Color (Yellow) -
2{3-3} skeins
☐ Contrasting Color (Black) -
1{1-2} skein(s)

## Knitting Needles
Straight,
☐ Size 6 (4 mm),
☐ Size 7 (4.5 mm) **and**
☐ Size 10 (6 mm) (for binding off )
Double pointed (set of 5),
☐ Size 7 (4.5 mm)
16" (40.5 cm) Circular,
☐ Size 7 (4.5 mm)
**or** sizes needed for gauge

## Additional Supplies
☐ Split ring marker
☐ Yarn needle

# DIAPER COVER

Work same as Basic Diaper Cover, page 2.

# BOOTIES

Work same as Basic Booties, page 3.

# HAT
## SIZE INFORMATION

| Size | Finished Circumference | |
|---|---|---|
| 0-3 Months | 12½" | (32 cm) |
| 3-6 Months | 14¼" | (36 cm) |
| 6-12 Months | 16" | (40.5 cm) |

*Size Note:* We have printed the instructions for the sizes in different colors to make it easier for you to find:

• 0-3 Months in Blue

• 3-6 Months in Pink

• 6-12 Months in Green

Instructions in Black apply to all sizes.

# GAUGE INFORMATION

With circular needle, in Stockinette Stitch (knit each rnd), 18 sts and 28 rnds = 4" (10 cm)

# TECHNIQUES USED

Knit in front and back increase *(Figs. 5a & b, page 29)*

K2 tog *(Fig. 6, page 29)*

# INSTRUCTIONS
## BODY

With 📹 circular needle and Yellow, cast on 56{64-72} sts **(Fig. 1, page 28)**; 📹 place a marker to indicate the beginning of the round **(see Markers, page 28)**.

Knit 11{11-13} rnds.

Drop unused color to **wrong** side to be carried at the back of work.

Drop Yellow; with Black knit 6{7-8} rnds.

Drop Black; with Yellow knit 6{7-8} rnds.

Repeat last 12{14-16} rounds.

Cut Yellow.

## SHAPING

Change to 📹 double pointed needles **(Fig. 2, page 28)** when there are too few stitches to use the circular needle.

**Rnd 1:** With Black, (K6, K2 tog) around: 49{56-63} sts.

**Rnd 2:** Knit around.

**Rnd 3:** (K5, K2 tog) around: 42{48-54} sts.

**Rnd 4:** Knit around.

**Rnd 5:** (K4, K2 tog) around: 35{40-45} sts.

**Rnd 6:** Knit around.

**Rnd 7:** (K3, K2 tog) around: 28{32-36} sts.

**Rnd 8:** Knit around.

**Rnd 9:** (K2, K2 tog) around: 21{24-27} sts.

**Rnd 10:** Knit around.

**Rnd 11:** (K1, K2 tog) around: 14{16-18} sts.

**Rnd 12:** K2 tog around: 7{8-9} sts.

Cut yarn leaving a long end for sewing. 📹 To gather the remaining sts, thread the yarn needle with the end and slip the remaining sts onto the yarn needle and yarn, pull tightly to close the hole and secure end.

## ANTENNA

Flatten the hat with the front facing. Using a double pointed needle and Black, 📹 pick up 4 sts at side edge **(Fig. 9b, page 30)**, 1" (2.5 cm) from the gathered sts at top.

Make an 📹 I-Cord as follows: ★ Without turning the needle, slide the sts to the opposite end of the needle, K4; repeat from ★ until the I-Cord measures approximately 2{3-4}"/5{7.5-10} cm.

**Increase Row:** Knit in front and back of each st across: 8 sts.

**Last Row:** Turn; purl across.

Cut yarn leaving a long end for sewing. Thread the yarn needle with the end and slip the remaining sts onto the yarn needle and yarn, pull tightly to close the hole and secure end; insert needle down through the center of the I-Cord to hide end and to help the Antenna to stand upright.

Repeat on opposite side.

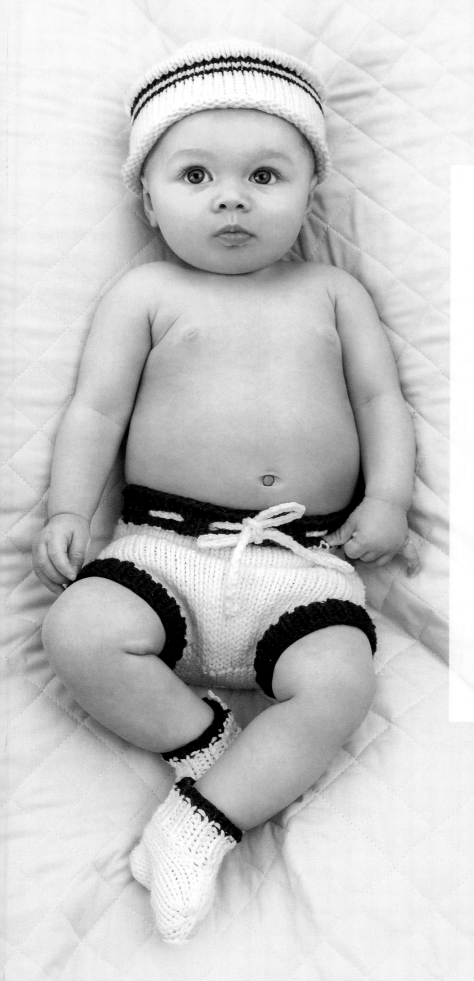

# Sailor

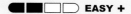 **EASY +**

## SHOPPING LIST

------------------------------------------------

### Yarn (Medium Weight) 🧶 MEDIUM 4
**[1.75 ounces, 80 yards (50 grams, 73 meters) per skein]:**
- ☐ Main Color (White) - 2{3-3} skeins
- ☐ Contrasting Color (Navy) - 1 skein

### Knitting Needles
Straight,
- ☐ Size 6 (4 mm),
- ☐ Size 7 (4.5 mm) **and**
- ☐ Size 10 (6 mm) (for binding off)

Double pointed (set of 5),
- ☐ Size 7 (4.5 mm)

16" (40.5 cm) Circular,
- ☐ Size 6 (4 mm) **and**
- ☐ Size 7 (4.5 mm)
  **or** sizes needed for gauge

### Additional Supplies
- ☐ Split ring marker
- ☐ Yarn needle

# DIAPER COVER

Work same as Basic Diaper Cover, page 2.

# BOOTIES

Work same as Basic Booties, page 3.

# HAT
## SIZE INFORMATION

| Size | Finished Circumference | |
|---|---|---|
| 0-3 Months | 12½" | (32 cm) |
| 3-6 Months | 14¼" | (36 cm) |
| 6-12 Months | 16" | (40.5 cm) |

*Size Note:* We have printed the instructions for the sizes in different colors to make it easier for you to find:

• 0-3 Months in Blue

• 3-6 Months in Pink

• 6-12 Months in Green

Instructions in Black apply to all sizes.

# GAUGE INFORMATION

With larger size circular needle, in Stockinette Stitch (knit each rnd), 18 sts and 28 rnds = 4" (10 cm)

# TECHNIQUE USED

K2 tog *(Fig. 6, page 29)*

# INSTRUCTIONS

## BRIM

With smaller size 📹 circular needle and White, leaving a long end for sewing, cast on 64{72-80} sts *(Fig. 1, page 28)*; 📌 place a marker to indicate the beginning of the round *(see Markers, page 28)*.

Knit 7 rnds.

Drop unused color to **wrong** side to be carried at the back of work.

Drop White; with Navy, knit 2{2-3} rnds.

Drop Navy; with White, knit 2{2-3} rnds.

Drop White; with Navy, knit 2{2-3} rnds.

Cut Navy; with White, knit 8{10-12} rnds.

**Next Rnd:** ★ K6{7-8}, K2 tog; repeat from ★ around: 56{64-72} sts.

## BODY

**Rnd 1:** Using larger size circular needle, knit around.

**Rnd 2:** Slip 1 as if to **purl**, with yarn in front, slip st back to left point, turn work; knit around.

You are now working in the opposite direction with the **right** side of the Body facing. The Brim will be turned up.

Knit each rnd until Body measures approximately 4{4½-5}"/ 10{11.5-12.5} cm from Brim.

## SHAPING

Change to 📹 double pointed needles *(Fig. 2, page 28)* when there are too few stitches to use the circular needle.

**Rnd 1:** (K6, K2 tog) around: 49{56-63} sts.

**Rnd 2:** Knit around.

**Rnd 3:** (K5, K2 tog) around: 42{48-54} sts.

**Rnd 4:** Knit around.

**Rnd 5:** (K4, K2 tog) around: 35{40-45} sts.

**Rnd 6:** Knit around.

**Rnd 7:** (K3, K2 tog) around: 28{32-36} sts.

**Rnd 8:** Knit around.

**Rnd 9:** (K2, K2 tog) around: 21{24-27} sts.

**Rnd 10:** Knit around.

**Rnd 11:** (K1, K2 tog) around: 14{16-18} sts.

**Rnd 12:** K2 tog around: 7{8-9} sts.

Cut yarn leaving a long end for sewing. 📹 To gather the remaining sts, thread the yarn needle with the end and slip the remaining sts onto the yarn needle and yarn; pull tightly to close the hole and secure end.

To form hem, fold cast on edge to **wrong** side of Brim and sew in place to first Navy rnd.

Fold Brim up.

# Work Sock

**■■□□** EASY +

## SHOPPING LIST

-----------------------------------

### Yarn (Medium Weight) [MEDIUM 4]
[3 ounces, 145 yards
(85 grams, 133 meters) per skein]:
- ☐ Main Color (Grey) - 2{3-3} skeins

[3.5 ounces, 170 yards
(100 grams, 156 meters) per skein]:
- ☐ Contrasting Color (Cream) -
  1 skein
- ☐ Trim (Red) - small amount

### Knitting Needles
Straight,
- ☐ Size 6 (4 mm),
- ☐ Size 7 (4.5 mm) **and**
- ☐ Size 10 (6 mm) (for binding off)

Double pointed (set of 5),
- ☐ Size 7 (4.5 mm)

16" (40.5 cm) Circular,
- ☐ Size 7 (4.5 mm)
  **or** sizes needed for gauge

### Additional Supplies
- ☐ Split ring marker
- ☐ Yarn needle

# DIAPER COVER

Work same as Basic Diaper Cover, page 2, binding off Waistband and Leg Ribbings with Red.

# BOOTIES

Work same as Basic Booties, page 3, binding off Cuff with Red.

# HAT
## SIZE INFORMATION

| Size | Finished Circumference | |
|---|---|---|
| 0-3 Months | 12½" | (32 cm) |
| 3-6 Months | 14¼" | (36 cm) |
| 6-12 Months | 16" | (40.5 cm) |

*Size Note:* We have printed the instructions for the sizes in different colors to make it easier for you to find:

• 0-3 Months in Blue

• 3-6 Months in Purple

• 6-12 Months in Green

Instructions in Black apply to all sizes.

# GAUGE INFORMATION

With circular needle,
in Stockinette Stitch (knit each rnd),
18 sts and 28 rnds = 4" (10 cm)

# TECHNIQUE USED

K2 tog *(Fig. 6, page 29)*

# INSTRUCTIONS

## RIBBING

With 📹 circular needle and Red, cast on 56{64-72} sts *(Fig. 1, page 28)*; 📹 place a marker to indicate the beginning of the round *(see Markers, page 28)*.

**Rnd 1:** (K1, P1) around.

Cut Red; with Cream, repeat Rnd 1 until piece measures approximately 1{1½-2}"/2.5{4-5} cm from cast on edge.

Cut Cream.

## BODY

With Grey, knit each rnd until piece measures approximately 5{6-7}"/12.5{15-18} cm from cast on edge.

## SHAPING

Change to 📹 double pointed needles *(Fig. 2, page 28)* when there are too few stitches to use the circular needle.

**Rnd 1:** (K6, K2 tog) around: 49{56-63} sts.

**Rnd 2:** Knit around.

**Rnd 3:** (K5, K2 tog) around: 42{48-54} sts.

**Rnd 4:** Knit around.

**Rnd 5:** (K4, K2 tog) around: 35{40-45} sts.

**Rnd 6:** Knit around.

**Rnd 7:** (K3, K2 tog) around: 28{32-36} sts.

**Rnd 8:** Knit around.

**Rnd 9:** (K2, K2 tog) around: 21{24-27} sts.

**Rnd 10:** Knit around.

**Rnd 11:** (K1, K2 tog) around: 14{16-18} sts.

**Rnd 12:** K2 tog around: 7{8-9} sts.

### SIZE 0-3 MONTHS ONLY

**Rnd 13:** K1, K2 tog around: 4 sts.

### SIZE 3-6 MONTHS ONLY

**Rnd 13:** K2 tog around: 4 sts.

### SIZE 6-12 MONTHS ONLY

**Rnd 13:** K1, K2 tog around: 5 sts.

**Rnd 14:** K2 tog, K3: 4 sts.

### ALL SIZES

Slip remaining 4 sts onto one double pointed needle.

Make an 📹 I-Cord as follows:
★ Without turning the needle, slide the sts to the opposite end of the needle, K4; repeat from ★ until the I-Cord measures approximately 4" (10 cm).

Cut Grey; with Red, work 2 rows.

Cut yarn leaving a long end for sewing. 📹 To gather the remaining sts, thread the yarn needle with the end and slip the remaining sts onto the yarn needle and yarn, pull tightly to close the hole and secure end; insert needle down through the center of the I-Cord to hide end.

Tie I-Cord in a knot.

# General Instructions

## ABBREVIATIONS

| | |
|---|---|
| cm | centimeters |
| K | knit |
| mm | millimeters |
| P | purl |
| Rnd(s) | Round(s) |
| st(s) | stitch(es) |
| tog | together |
| YO | yarn over |

## SYMBOLS & TERMS

★ — work instructions following ★ as many **more** times as indicated in addition to the first time.

( ) or [ ] — work enclosed instructions **as many** times as specified by the number immediately following **or** contains explanatory remarks.

colon (:) — the number(s) given after a colon at the end of a row or round denote(s) the number of stitches you should have on that row or round.

## GAUGE

Exact gauge is **essential** for proper fit. Before beginning your project, make a sample swatch in the yarn and needle specified in the individual instructions. After completing the swatch, measure it, counting your stitches and rows carefully. If your swatch is larger or smaller than specified, **make another, changing needle size to get the correct gauge**. Keep trying until you find the size needle(s) that will give you the specified gauge.

### KNIT TERMINOLOGY

| UNITED STATES | INTERNATIONAL |
|---|---|
| gauge = | tension |
| bind off = | cast off |
| yarn over (YO) = | yarn forward (yfwd) **or** yarn around needle (yrn) |

| Yarn Weight Symbol & Names | LACE 0 | SUPER FINE 1 | FINE 2 | LIGHT 3 | MEDIUM 4 | BULKY 5 | SUPER BULKY 6 |
|---|---|---|---|---|---|---|---|
| Type of Yarns in Category | Fingering, size 10 crochet thread | Sock, Fingering, Baby | Sport, Baby | DK, Light Worsted | Worsted, Afghan, Aran | Chunky, Craft, Rug | Bulky, Roving |
| Knit Gauge Range* in Stockinette St to 4" (10 cm) | 33-40** sts | 27-32 sts | 23-26 sts | 21-24 sts | 16-20 sts | 12-15 sts | 6-11 sts |
| Advised Needle Size Range | 000-1 | 1 to 3 | 3 to 5 | 5 to 7 | 7 to 9 | 9 to 11 | 11 and larger |

*GUIDELINES ONLY: The chart above reflects the most commonly used gauges and needle sizes for specific yarn categories.

** Lace weight yarns are usually knitted on larger needles to create lacy openwork patterns. Accordingly, a gauge range is difficult to determine. Always follow the gauge stated in your pattern.

| KNITTING NEEDLES | | | | | | | | | | | | | | | | | | |
|---|---|---|---|---|---|---|---|---|---|---|---|---|---|---|---|---|---|---|
| U.S. | 0 | 1 | 2 | 3 | 4 | 5 | 6 | 7 | 8 | 9 | 10 | 10½ | 11 | 13 | 15 | 17 | 19 | 35 | 50 |
| U.K. | 13 | 12 | 11 | 10 | 9 | 8 | 7 | 6 | 5 | 4 | 3 | 2 | 1 | 00 | 000 | --- | --- | --- | --- |
| Metric - mm | 2 | 2.25 | 2.75 | 3.25 | 3.5 | 3.75 | 4 | 4.5 | 5 | 5.5 | 6 | 6.5 | 8 | 9 | 10 | 12.75 | 15 | 19 | 25 |

| | |
|---|---|
| ■□□□ BEGINNER | Projects for first-time knitters using basic knit and purl stitches. Minimal shaping. |
| ■■□□ EASY | Projects using basic stitches, repetitive stitch patterns, simple color changes, and simple shaping and finishing. |
| ■■■□ INTERMEDIATE | Projects with a variety of stitches, such as basic cables and lace, simple intarsia, double-pointed needles and knitting in the round needle techniques, mid-level shaping and finishing. |
| ■■■■ EXPERIENCED | Projects using advanced techniques and stitches, such as short rows, fair isle, more intricate intarsia, cables, lace patterns, and numerous color changes. |

## MARKERS

As a convenience to you, we have used markers to mark the beginning of a round. Place a marker as instructed. You may use a purchased marker or tie a length of contrasting color yarn around the needle. When you reach a marker on each round, slip it from the left needle to the right needle; remove it when no longer needed.

When using double pointed needles, a split-ring marker can be placed around the first stitch in the round to indicate the beginning of the round. Move it up as the first stitch of each round is worked.

## CIRCULAR NEEDLE

When you knit a tube, you are going to work around on the outside of the circle, with the **right** side of the knitting facing you.

Using a circular needle, cast on all stitches as instructed. Untwist and straighten the stitches on the needle to be sure that the cast on ridge lays on the inside of the needle and never rolls around the needle.

Hold the needle so that the skein of yarn is attached to the stitch closest to the right hand point. Place a marker on the right hand point to mark the beginning of the round *(Fig. 1)*.

To begin working in the round, knit the stitches on the left hand point. Continue working each round as instructed without turning the work.

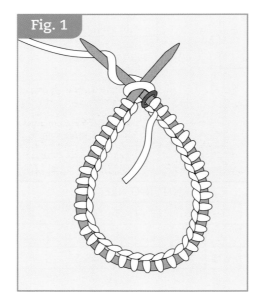

Fig. 1

## DOUBLE POINTED NEEDLES

When working too few stitches to use a circular needle, double pointed needles are required. Divide the stitches into fourths and slip one-fourth of the stitches onto each of 4 double pointed needles, forming a square *(Fig. 2)*.

With the fifth needle, work across the stitches on the first needle. You will now have an empty needle with which to work the stitches from the next needle. Work the first stitch of each needle firmly to prevent gaps.

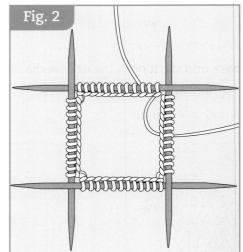

Fig. 2

## YARN OVER
### *(abbreviated YO)*

Bring the yarn forward **between** the needles, then back **over** the top of the right hand needle, so that it is now in position to knit the next stitch *(Fig. 3)*.

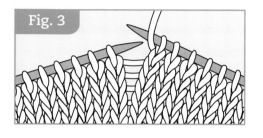
Fig. 3

## ADD ON NEW STITCHES

Insert the right needle into the stitch as if to **knit**, yarn over and pull loop through *(Fig. 4a)*, insert left needle into loop just worked from **front** to **back** and slip it onto the left needle *(Fig. 4b)*. Repeat for the required number of stitches.

Fig. 4a
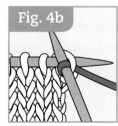
Fig. 4b

## KNIT IN FRONT & BACK INCREASE

Knit the next stitch but do **not** slip the old stitch off the left needle *(Fig. 5a)*. Insert the right needle into the **back** loop of the **same** stitch and knit it *(Fig. 5b)*, then slip the old stitch off the left needle.

Fig. 5a
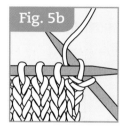
Fig. 5b

## KNIT 2 TOGETHER
### *(abbreviated K2 tog)*

Insert the right needle into the **front** of the first two stitches on the left needle as if to **knit** *(Fig. 6)*, then **knit** them together as if they were one stitch.

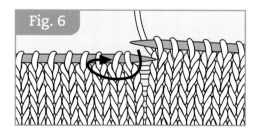
Fig. 6

## PURL 2 TOGETHER
### *(abbreviated P2 tog)*

Insert the right needle into the **front** of the first two stitches on the left needle as if to **purl** *(Fig. 7)*, then **purl** them together as if they were one stitch.

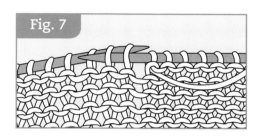
Fig. 7

## WEAVING SEAMS

Weaving can be used to join the ends of rows or the cast on edges of two pieces in a manner that appears to be seamless.

## END OF ROWS

With the **right** side of both pieces facing you and edges even, sew through both sides once to secure the beginning of the seam. Insert the yarn needle under the bar between the first and second stitches on the row and pull the yarn through **(Fig. 8a)**. Insert the yarn needle under the next bar on the second side. Repeat from side to side, being careful to match rows. If the edges are different lengths, it may be necessary to insert the needle under two bars at one edge.

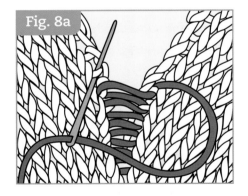

Fig. 8a

## CAST ON EDGES

With the **right** side of both pieces facing you and matching the cast on edges, bring the yarn needle from behind the work and through the center of the first stitch. ★ Bring the yarn needle over the top of the cast on stitches and insert it under both loops of the corresponding stitch on the second side **(Fig. 8b)**. Bring the yarn needle back over the cast on stitches and insert it under the inverted V of the next stitch **(Fig. 8c)**. Repeat from ★ across. Pull the yarn gently every 2 or 3 stitches, being careful to maintain even tension.

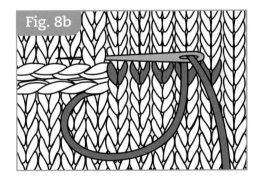

Fig. 8b

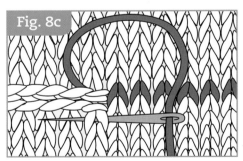

Fig. 8c

## PICKING UP STITCHES

When instructed to pick up stitches, insert the needle from the **front** to the **back** under two strands at the edge of the worked piece **(Fig. 9a)**. Put the yarn around the needle as if to **knit**, then bring the needle with the yarn back through the stitch to the right side, resulting in a stitch on the needle.

Repeat this along the edge, picking up the required number of stitches.

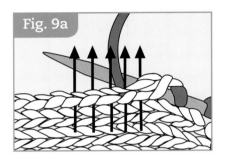

Fig. 9a

When instructed to pick up stitches for the Butterfly Antenna, page 20, insert the needle under two strands of a stitch **(Fig. 9b)**. Put the yarn around the needle as if to knit, then bring the needle with the yarn back through the stitch to the right side, resulting in a stitch on the needle.

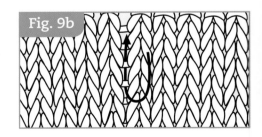

Fig. 9b

# EMBROIDERY STITCHES
## STRAIGHT STITCH

Straight stitch is just what the name implies, a single, straight stitch and can be used to form a star. Come up at odd numbers and go down at even numbers *(Fig. 10)*.

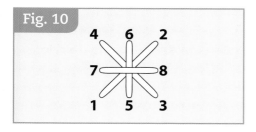

Fig. 10

## SATIN STITCH

Satin stitch is a series of straight stitches worked side by side so they touch but do not overlap. Come up at odd numbers and go down at even numbers *(Fig. 11)*.

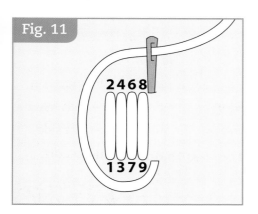

Fig. 11

# FRENCH KNOT

Bring needle up at 1. Wrap yarn around the needle the desired number of times and insert needle at 2, holding end of yarn with non-stitching fingers *(Fig. 12)*. Tighten the knot; then pull the needle through, holding yarn until it must be released.

Fig. 12

# DUPLICATE STITCH

Duplicate stitch is worked on Stockinette Stitch. Each knit stitch forms a V and you want to completely cover that V, so that the seed appears to have been knit into the piece.

Thread a yarn needle with an 18" (45.5 cm) length of yarn. With **right** side facing, bring the needle up from the **wrong** side at the base of the V, leaving an end to be woven in later (never tie knots). The needle should always go between the strands of yarn. Follow the right side of the V up and insert the needle from **right** to **left** under the legs of the V immediately above it, keeping the yarn on top of the stitch *(Fig. 13a)*, and draw through. Follow the left side of the V back down to the base and insert the needle back through the bottom of the same stitch where the first stitch began *(Fig. 13b, Duplicate Stitch completed)*.

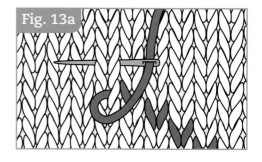

Fig. 13a

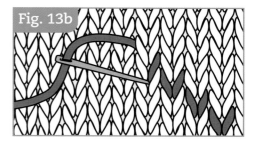

Fig. 13b

# Yarn Information

The sets in this book were made using a medium weight yarn with a bulky novelty yarn used for the embroidery on the Butterfly & Clouds. Any brand of medium weight yarn may be used. It is best to refer to the yardage/meters when determining how many skeins or balls to purchase. Remember, to arrive at the finished size, it is the GAUGE/TENSION that is important, not the brand of yarn.

For your convenience, listed below are the colors used to create our photography models.

### STARS & MOON
*Bernat® Handicrafter® Cotton*
Navy - #13114 Indigo
White - #00001 White
Yellow - #00030 Pale Yellow

### WATERMELON
*Bernat® Handicrafter® Cotton*
Red - #13530 Country Red
Green - #13712 Hot Green
White - #00001 White
Black - #13040 Black Licorice

### COW
*Bernat® Handicrafter® Cotton*
White - #00001 White
Black - #13040 Black Licorice

### BUTTERFLY & CLOUDS
*Bernat® Handicrafter® Cotton*
Blue - #00010 French Blue
White - #00001 White
Yellow - #00030 Pale Yellow
Black - #13040 Black Licorice
*Red Heart® Baby Clouds™*
White - #9311 Cloud

### BUMBLE BEE
*Bernat® Handicrafter® Cotton*
Yellow - #00030 Pale Yellow
Black - #13040 Black Licorice

### SAILOR
*Bernat® Handicrafter® Cotton*
White - #00001 White
Navy - #13114 Indigo

### WORK SOCK
*Lion Brand® Vanna's Choice®*
Grey - #405 Silver Heather
Red - #113 Scarlet
*Lion Brand® Vanna's Choice® Baby*
Cream - #098 Lamb

## Meet the Designer
## Lee Ann Garrett

"My love for knitting small things and embellishing has led me to design these fun and different baby designs," Lee Ann Garrett says.

"My grandmother put my first set of knitting needles in my hands when I was just 10 years old. I designed and knit my own Barbie doll clothes using scraps of fur and sequins to decorate them."

She's been designing baby hats for 12 years now. "I started with a couple of fruit hats and it has grown into 40 original designs. I have turned it into a full-time business and sell my hats at local farmer's markets, craft shows, specialty boutiques, and on-line."

To see more of Lee Ann's designs, visit her Farm Fresh Knits shop at www.farmfreshknits.etsy.com.

The retired registered nurse lives with her husband and dog in Ontario, Canada. Other interests include playing guitar, singing in a choir, and outdoor sports such as skiing, skating, camping, and canoeing.

We have made every effort to ensure that these instructions are accurate and complete. We cannot, however, be responsible for human error, typographical mistakes, or variations in individual work.

Production Team: Instructional/Technical Writer - Cathy Hardy; Editorial Writer - Susan Frantz Wiles; Senior Graphic Artist - Lora Puls; Graphic Artist - Jessica Bramlett; Photo Stylist - Sondra Daniel; and Photographer - Ken West.